presents

JEFF KOONS

By Rainald Goetz

Translated by David Tushingham

First performed at The Drum, Theatre Royal, Plymouth 13th October 2004

Jeff Koons is supported by The Linbury Trust and Goethe Institut, London

This translation was commissioned with the help of an Arts Council England Theatre Writing Translation Commission Award

JEFF KOONS

By Rainald Goetz

Translated by David Tushingham

Cast
Andrew Dennis
Danielle King
Nazim Kourgli
Louise Ludgate
Jonathan McGuinness

Director Gordon Anderson
Designer Becs Andrews
Associate Director Dan O'Neill
Lighting Designer Mark Howland
Production Manager Tom Albu
Company Stage Manager Marius Ronning
Technical Stage Manager Mark Howland
Wardrobe Supervisor Laura Smith
Design Intern Elizabeth Swartz

Press Agent Anne Mayer
Graphic Design Mark Goddard

Executive Producer Emma Dunton
Administrator Jenni Kershaw

Set built by KW Props and Sets

With special thanks to: Simon Sturgess, Upstage Event Management, David Nagle and William Kallaway at Kallaway ltd, Sylviana Ollennu and Claudia Amthor-Croft at the Goethe Institut London. We would also like to thank Esther Firman for knitwear and Hollie Maddox for screen printing.

Biographies

Tom Albu Production Manager

Tom trained at the Bristol Old Vic Theatre School before working as a Stage Manager for various companies including two years with Theatre de Complicite. Ten years as a production manager includes work for Cheek By Jowl, Music Theatre London, The Bush Theatre, Slava Polunin's *SNOWSHOW*, Method & Madness, Tamasha, The Shout, Trestle, Tête à Tête, Royal College of Music, Aldeburgh Productions and New Kent Opera. He was also Production Manager and Lighting Designer for The Right Size's Olivier Award winning show *Do You Come Here Often?* Previously for ATC, Tom production managed *Venus and Adonis* and *Macbeth False Memories*.

Gordon Anderson Director

Gordon is Artistic Director of ATC for whom he has directed *Country Music, One Minute, Out of Our Heads, Arabian Night* and *In the Solitude of Cotton Fields*. Other theatre credits include: *Great Expectations* (Old Vic, Bristol); *Bluebird* (Royal Court); *The Threesome* (Lyric Hammersmith); *The Reckless are Dying Out*; *The Grand Ceremonial* (both Lyric Studio); *Manon* (ETO); *Hansel and Gretel* (Scottish Opera); *The Mikado* (Grange Park Opera); *The Silver Lake* (Wilton's Music Hall), *The Rib Cage* (Manchester Royal Exchange) and *Outside On the Street* (Gate Theatre). As a director of comedy he has directed *Catherine Tate*, *The League of Gentlemen*, *Navelgazing*, *Conversations with My Agent* and projects for the *Channel 4 Sitcom Festival*. He recently directed *The Catherine Tate Show* for Tiger Aspect/BBC2

Becs Andrews Designer

Becs studied theatre design at Wimbledon School of Art and Fine Art at the Ruskin School of Fine Art and Drawing. Theatre and Opera designs include: *Twelfth Night* (English Touring Theatre), *Perpetua* (Latchmere Theatre), *What Became of the Witch?* (Theatre and Beyond tour), *The Magic Flute* (Opera Oxford), and *West Side Story* (Oxford Playhouse). Dance designs include: *Set and Reset* (EDge European tour), *Clepsydra, Lounge* (The Place), *Twos* (St. Pancras Church Crypt), *Corner of the World* (Performing Arts Research and Training Studios, Rosas, Brussels). Becs won the overall prize in the Linbury Biennial Prize for Stage Design 2003 for her design for *Jeff Koons*.

Andrew Dennis Cast

Andrew trained at Mountview Academy of Theatre Arts. His theatre credits include: *Bouncers* (Hull/West End); *Wonderful Town* (Grange Park Opera); *Bluebird* (Royal Court); *Une Tempete* (Gate); *The Boys From Syracuse* (Sheffield Crucible); *'Tis A Pity She's A Whore* (Talawa). Andrew also performed with the RSC for 18 months appearing in numerous productions including: *A Midsummer Night's Dream, Tales From Ovid* and *Timon of Athens*. Television includes: *Doctors, The Bill, Down To Earth, Jeffrey Archer – The Truth, Redcap, My Hero, Dream Team, Hidden Camera, Hale and Pace, Trevor McDonald Tonight, Dyke Blend, Roger Roger,* and *Shelley.*

Emma Dunton Executive Producer

Since joining ATC in 2001 Emma has produced *In the Solitude of Cotton-Fields* by Bernard-Marie Koltes, *Arabian Night* by Roland Schimmelpfennig, *Out of Our Heads* by Susan Earl and Janice Phayre, *One Minute* by Simon Stephens, *Excuses!* by Joel Joan and Jordi Sanchez and *Country Music* by Simon Stephens. At Volcano Theatre Company Emma produced and managed the national and international tours of *Macbeth-Director's Cut, The Town That Went Mad* and *Private Lives*. Previously she has worked at the British Council and on feature films in Los Angeles.

Rainald Goetz Writer

Rainald Goetz was born in Munich in 1954. He has gained doctorates in both medicine and history. He lives and works as a freelance writer in Berlin. Prizes and awards include: Author Prize of *The Kranich with the Stone* (1983); Suhrkamp Author Scholarship (1983); Work Scholarship for Berlin Writers (1983); Demand Prize of the City Muechen (1984); Mulheimer Dramatist prize for *War* (1988); Promotion gift of the Schillerpreises of the country Baden-Wuerttemberg (1989); Heinrich Boell prize of the city Cologne (1991); Muelheimer dramatist prize for *Qatar Act* (1993); Prize of the Peter Suhrkamp donation (1995); Else Lasker pupil prize of the country Rhineland-Palatinate (1999); Mulheimer dramatist prize for *Jeff Koons* (2000); William Raabe prize for *Waste for All* (2000) Plays include: *War* (1987), *Slaughter* (1988), *Colic* (1988*), Fortress* (1992), *Qatar Act* (1992), *Critism in Fortress* (1993*), Jeff Koons* (1999), *Err* (2000), *Rave* (2001)

Mark Howland Lighting Designer and Technical Stage Manager

Theatre work was far from Mark's mind when he embarked on a degree at Oxford University. However, after stumbling across the Oxford Playhouse and having lit many student productions, he went on to study Stage Lighting at RADA. Other lighting designs include *The Magic Flute, The Pirates of Penzance,* and *Guys & Dolls* (at the Nuffield Theatre), *An Audience with Sid & Nancy* (Etcetera Theatre), *Problem Child* (New End Theatre), *Many a Slipped, Twixt, Cap and Dick* (Lilian Baylis Theatre, Sadler's Wells) and *Caligula* (Battersea Arts Centre). Mark's portfolio can be seen on the internet at: www.markhowland.co.uk

Jenni Kershaw Administrator

Jenni joined ATC in May 2003 whilst completing her MA in Arts Administration and Cultural Policy at Goldsmiths College, University of London. Previously she gained a BA in English Literature and Theology at

Liverpool University (Chester College) whilst gaining work experience at The Gateway Theatre in Chester.

Danielle King Cast

Danielle's theatre credits include: *The Rivals* (Compass National Tour); *Two Gentlemen of Verona* (Northcott, Exeter); *As You Like It* (Sphinx Tour); *Sleeping Beauty* (Young Vic); *The Taming of the Shrew* (Salisbury Playhouse); *Trance* (White Bear); *On the Razzle* (Chichester Festival); *Richard II* and *Coriolanus* (Almeida/Gainsborough); *The Art of Success* (The Studio). Television credits include: *Bad Girls* (series 2, 3 and 5), *Holby City* and *Ultimate Force*. Film credit: *The Gathering Storm* (Labrador Films).

Nazim Kourgli Cast

Nazim trained at the Welsh College of Music and Drama. Theatre credits include *Once A Catholic* (New Victoria, Stoke) and *Romeo and Juliet* (Liverpool Playhouse). Television credits include *Ultimate Force* (ITV).

Louise Ludgate Cast

Louise trained at the Royal Scottish Academy of Music and Drama. Most recent theatre credits include: *When the Dons were Kings* (The Lemon Tree, Aberdeen); *Iron* (Traverse, Edinburgh/Royal Court, London); *Lament* (Suspect Culture); *Casanova* (Suspect Culture); *Greta* (Traverse, Edinburgh). Television credits include: *Taggart* (SMG); *Spooks* (BBC); *Glasgow Kiss* (BBC). Recent films include: *No Man's Land* (Hopscotch Films Ltd), *Goodbye Happy Ending* (Fallingwater Films) and *Café Rendevous* (Screenworks). Louise has also worked for BBC Radio Scotland and appeared in many plays for BBC Radio 3.

Jonathan McGuinness Cast

Jonathan McGuinness trained at Central School of Speech and Drama. Theatre includes: For Ed Hall's Propeller Company *A Midsummer Night's Dream* (Comedy Theatre, West End and New York); *Rose Rage* (Haymarket Theatre, West End); *Twelfth Night*, *Henry V* (world tour); *Comedy of Errors* (world tour). Other work: *Richard III* (Sheffield Crucible); *The Last Valentine* (Almeida); *Mojo* (Sheffield Crucible); *Crazy Horse* (Paines Plough); *Corner Boys* (Royal Court); *The Knocky* (Royal Court); *The Catherine Tate Show* (Edinburgh). TV: *The Catherine Tate Show* (BBC series); *In Search of the Brontes* (BBC); *A Touch of Frost, The Bill, Get Calf – Six Sides of Coogan, Game On, Poldark, Crown Prosecutor, Sharpe's Gold,* and *Have Your Cake and Eat It.*

Dan O'Neill Associate Director

Trained at London Contemporary Dance School, Dan has choreographed for film, TV and theatre. His short film, *The Linesman,* broadcast on BBC 2 and 3, has been screened at film festivals world wide, including Paris, New York, Rio and Hong Kong. His most recent stage choreography includes

Escapade (The South Bank Centre), *Great Expectations* (Bristol Old Vic), Peepshow (Frantic Assembly). Dan is a founder member of Lea Anderson's award winning Featherstonehaughs and has performed with many other leading companies including DV8, Extemporary, Second Stride and Toronto Dance Theatre. He has led many residencies, workshops and dance/film projects with actors, dancers, teachers and young people, both in the UK and abroad.

Marius Ronning Company Stage Manager

Marius graduated from RADA in 2001 where he trained as a Stage Manager. Since then he has been working freelance. He has worked for Trestle (Mask). Tete a Tete (Opera), Royal College of Music (Opera), New Kent Opera, English Touring Opera, Wee (Dance) and ATC. Marius has worked on UK tours and has experience of working in Italy, France and Norway.

Laura Smith Wardrobe Designer

After graduating from the Theatre Design Course at Wimbledon School of Art in 2002, Laura went on to London College of Fashion to study Bespoke Tailoring. On completion of the course she trained at a large London costume house as a Period Costumier. In March 2004 Laura co-designed a short film, *Heel* directed by Diego Arredondo that premiered at the Cannes Film Festival in the Straight8 Competition. Following this she has worked as Costume Assistant to Maja Meschede on *Puritain,* written and directed by Hadi Haijaig and produced by Parliament Films. It will be due for general release in 2005.

David Tushingham Translator

David Tushingham is a dramaturg for the Theater der Welt Festival 2005 and the Stuttgart State Theatre. He has translated *Arabian Night* for ATC and numerous plays for the Royal Court Theatre including *Mr. Kolpert*, *Waiting Room Germany* and *Stranger's House*. He has also adapted Salman Rushdie's *Haroun and the Sea of Stories* for the Royal National Theatre and most recently translated *The Woman Before* by Roland Schimmelpfennig.

ατc

ATC was founded in 1979 to tour innovative work throughout the UK. Over the years the company has developed a tradition of ensemble excellence and a reputation for originality and internationalism, picking up many awards along the way. Since Gordon Anderson and Emma Dunton joined the company in 2001 ATC has focused upon contemporary work and forged dynamic partnerships with companies and artists from across the world.

ATC recently produced two new plays by the award-winning playwright Simon Stephens: *Country Music* in a co-production with the Royal Court in June 2004; and *One Minute* in a co-production with Sheffield Crucible Theatre, which went on a national tour before arriving at the Bush Theatre in London in February 2004. Other recent productions include the English language premieres of *Excuses!* by Jordi Sanchez and Joel Joan directed by David Grindley (in a co-production with the Barcelona-based company Krampack) and *Arabian Night* by Roland Schimmelpfennig – both shows toured the UK and played at Soho Theatre in London. ATC has also worked with comedy writer-performers Susan & Janice developing their hit show *Out of Our Heads* and produced Bernard Marie Koltes' *In the Solitude of Cotton Fields* in a site-specific performance at the disused Aldwych Underground station on the Strand.

In the autumn 2004 *Jeff Koons* tours to The Drum, Plymouth; Merlin Theatre, Frome; Quay Arts, Isle of Wight; The Traverse, Edinburgh; Birmingham Repertory Theatre and The Tobacco Factory in Bristol. The show will be performed at the ICA in London in November 2004.

ATC, Malvern House, 15-16 Nassau Street, London W1W 7AB
T: 0207 580 7723   F: 0207 580 7724
E: atc@atc-online.com www.atc-online.com

ATC is funded by Arts Council England

Rainald Goetz
JEFF KOONS
translated by David Tushingham

The full script of *Jeff Koons* follows.
In the ATC production, some sections were cut. Square
brackets denote sections cut in performance by ATC.

ACT THREE

'St John the Baptist, New York 1989'
– Jeff Koons

III: Palette

1. OUTSIDE

We won't get in there.
I will.
Yeah?
Come on.

2. AT THE DOOR

17 marks please.
For two?
Uh-uh, each. 33 for two.
33?
Uh-huh.
There you go.
You wanna stamp?
Nah.
Enjoy.
Thanks.

3. INSIDE

That was quick.
What now?
Bit crowded.
'Ts nice.

We wanted
to get filthy

painting
we wanted to be the ultimate.

I mentioned
in my talk
the significance of ceremony.

[4. WALL OF WORDS

It's good it's full. It's packed it's heaving. Covered with
me, rubbed up, steaming. Words carved in stone and
perfect sound. Everything brought out, disarmed,
exposed. Don't know how wrong, how much without.
Just paint and a warm coat. Your question, sure, towards
the end, but not the gap in the logic, the leap. We walk
for a bit, lie down, we dream, drink, carry on. Stones on
the wall, eyes like steel, faces hard too, a bit too hard. He
comes over, so does she, with that weird walk, like they're
on some invisible cord. He takes refuge in liquid softness,
next to that quiet skin, builds image and form out of
plasticene. Tired of conflict, get rid of the bad. Let
legitimate concerns take off the gloss, overcome
resistance, re-connect with rigour, then don't lose that
vigour, look after it. Wrap it in fur and tie it securely with
memories of past injustice. We go back, go on ahead, we
talk, drink, dance, laugh. Music under a low roof,
brightening the mind, all around at first, then returning
and now starting all over again. You've got to be careful
making judgements you don't, hang on. I can, I've lost, I
ought to calm down. One talks about before, another like
just now and from the back there's a wave of madness.
Not much, put it away. It's just you, we, how it. It had
to, that too, and you, and if I feel, a bit, don't know, like
we, she already, so did we, cocooned in what had gone
before. It was like that, and then? Trusting those who
watch over us, unprotected.]

5. LET THE BASS KICK

bum
cha bum
cha bum cha

I know

cha bumcha
bum bum
bum
cha bum

big time

da bum
cha bum
chabum cha
bum

fun
kind of yeah?
yeah

6. THE DANCEFLOOR

tousled and aroused
thrashed bashed hacked to bits
caught in the wind
seat of your pants
heading for the moon

it's shut
this one's open
in there
let's go

going ow
and ooh
all those ahs
what the

signed up, committed
thrashed bashed
totally –
yeah yeah, 's enough of that

7. AT THE BAR

We talk about
technology, graphics, construction.
The concept of the concrete.
A critique of politics.
Greatness, what language, what it means.
Debates, discussions. A dispute about method.
Painted words, what colour, what typeface.
Computer crashes, puppy, why others
won't be so lucky.
The new pictures tomorrow.
How big or small, sexualizing the space.
At in which from, ultimately these.
How you approach this, what leads to that. Which is
then exactly. Injury, violence. Ideas.
Escape, desire. Children, authority. Keeping
the depth plain and even, to keep learning.

And when's obviousness an effect
and when's it just moribund. And when are the sceptics
right
and when should you use neon colour effects?
We talk about questions and the talk
that energizes you. Maybe wrongly.
We're not very accurate, we know that.
It's about trying things out, grabbing them chucking them
around,
it's about future acts in the present moment.
About something that comes from us
opening ourselves up gradually towards it.

8. THE BACK

shall we take something else?
what've we got?
everything pretty much
yeah?
yeah
right
so?
what do you think?
dunno
what do you feel like?
huh, erm, dunno
less go back there
good idea

9. THE LOO

yeah but I'm not really
in love with him
I just think he's cute
he's good to get your hands on
clock em a bit
snog em a bit
then you can tell
if they're up to much
if it's going anywhere
maybe you're just
a bit horny for something
nothing wrong with that
is there?

This is the laboratory
and you're the guinea pig
for our ex-experiment

you mean, he's?
where?
I'll be right there
you go first
I'm all wet already

RAINALD GOETZ

[10. ON THE FLOOR

fag ends and ash
dirt and concrete
shoes and boots
women's feet

men's legs
trousers in shirts
hair in trousers
let it all go

start again
yeah

what, I can't hear you?
you angry?
no

soles and leather
techno and whips
drugs and lacquer
send me
I'll bend you

gimme the coke
we only just got here
I want a drag
you got another E

Peter and Peter
with Gabi, Yasmin
that one from last night
she was fit

any more?
why?
see you then
see you tomorrow

get up
get up and go
course, yes, be right there

not us
we're not
what?
sorry?
what
or what?
skin up again
then go to the bar]

11. THE WALL

And in front of him he sees something that's been seen
so often but never painted, an image of these
connections as they're moving, shadowy, dark, and yet
quite clear. Their structural forms. A bond and a bit of
bare flesh. An eye and a look. Thoughts of craving. Teeth,
lips, colours, just thinking in colours, no words at first,
think about words and the words come. A feeling for
relationships, distance and wanting, reflected in blinking,
in her withdrawing her hand. Her neck says look at me,
the smoking too. Her shrug, her pride, the rules of the
game. I don't understand, I do. I would if only. He could.
I don't want to, I don't know. I'm supposed to, with her.
Hang on, start again, let's be clear about this. The wall
with the shadows on it, the abstract mixture. A real
mixture, a normal reality. The act and the plan, the body,
the intention. How much of the plan can be seen? How's
intention revealed? The music breaks, it breaks in your
head, the sound's interrupted by this, it calls for logic and
melody. The whip, the rhythm, abstractly in: yeah what?
The correspondences and these stories, it must be
doable, in an image. And there's always: then what?
Yeah, right. Then what? That, of course, then this. He can
see it right in front of him, that's it.

RAINALD GOETZ

[12. CLOSE BY

warn, plead, resist, worry
crave, doubt, look out, hope

burden
melancholy
sympathy
guilt

poor, excluded, derided
frozen out, marginalized
the iron man
you've been seeing her

I go, take, wanted, went
we're healed of any buts
we're also the ones who didn't, aren't we

right, dancing, drinking, drinking beer
and let her quietly into the car that

concept
society
bar
banquette

structure
building
sculpture
site

sorrow, emptiness, reading, fear
get drunk, get sung to, smiled at, laugh,
danced, talked, stepped back, observed,
drunk, drink, dance, beer
and beauty, meadow, stars, here

with you
to me
to you to you]

13. GUEST LIST

THE YOUNG TURK
THE OLD FART
THE MIDDLE MAN

THE COOL CHICK
THE HOT FOX
THE WILD TIGRESS

JOHN THE BAPTIST
BOBBY ON THE BEAT
CUDDLY TOY

WRITERS
PAINTERS
MUSICIANS

PRESS
MONEY
PUBLIC

THE HIGH COURT
THE LAST JUDGEMENT
THE VERDICT

WORLD
SPACE
UNIVERSE

[14. THE LAST RESORT OF THE UNEMPLOYABLE: BAR WORK

a song of worries
a prayer to the night
bowed by the years
weighed down with sadness

past it
punished
disturbed
and peturbed

d'you miss her
sung softly

now that she
was never the
we want to re-

experiences
weren't so bad
actions
fun too

let's go
shout
we turn round

singing
to the night
shouted
in the face of trouble

refuelled too
at the same time

what they were like when they had hair
they're going to find out]

15. ON THE DOOR

sorry, regulars only tonight
my name's Wagner
never mind
I'm expected
where?
here
uh-huh
could you check?
what did you say your name was?
Wagner
Wagner?
yeah
sorry it's not here

that can't be right

why not?
I should be on there
Yeah, a lot of people think that
but you're not

it's got be a mistake

it's not
could you stop
blocking the way please?
so people can get in
are they all regulars?
are they?
if you really want to know
Mr?
Wagner
Wagner, you're pissing me off
and for that you can stay outside

you're gonna regret this

right
now will you please fuck off
you're getting in the way of me
doing my job

16. BEER PUMP

Not that he thinks it's worth repeating or disproving in
some brilliant way, what for, that'd be ridiculous.
Horrible. He was thinking more of a snapshot of the
situation, showing how fucked all these mediocrities are.
Without him being able to say how or what it's going to
be like exactly. And what the results will be. Permanent
failure, yeah, no. Look at them now. It's like they've all
expanded, there are more of them, they're heavier, more
powerful. Almost spherical, like him there, you couldn't
pick him up even if you wanted to. The voice of the grave,
you could call it. And all this stuff about the past,

questions whether, if you, where they were then. Those
who award the plaudits, where you're obliged to say, have
said: my life then and me now. How I, when I, without
you. Someone to confront this left-over reality, isolated
and radicalized, sharpened to a fine point. Not some do-
nothing, who couldn't whatever, it was you, no-one else.
Nothing you can do about that. Because what does it
mean, this I, this self? Was it ever a site to store bits and
pieces, to hack things apart and put them back together?
Now it's a state, one of destruction, chance encounters,
defined by what it's against, the outside, war internalized
as an existence in the margins, as that which is. And
what about creativity then? Because each in-the-now
moment ends and weighs itself against its immediate
predecessor, you're more or less having to fertilize a dead
spirit. Yeah, I think it is possible. That there's an answer,
so to speak. Where yeah, sure, reality is the supreme
authority, the big book that IS his mind, absolutely. And
then? Well following on from that, you could, maybe in a
way. Or possibly something else entirely. We'll see.

[17. COUNTER

good idea
that idea
idea of
a written concept
the quality of chatter
in praise of fleshliness
tell me a bit about

she tells about this time
when some woman says to the artist
excuse me I've got a question
go on
what can I do for you
when you were talking about no jobs

what's this about?
I was talking about what?
blowjobs?

talking about that interview
bringing up those questions
the idea
ever so slightly deliberate
all about
getting wet and stuff

that's out of order
something like that
there's no need
to do it like
is it really necessary?
no way]

18. ORDERING

talked, drank
danced, drank more

beer, beer
out of here

what sorry?
who did with who?

four beers
yeah
nice one

four beers, four beers
and a jug of cold

ok
don't worry
no problem, man

danced and drunk
drenched and driven
sculptures conceived

constructed finished
danced drunk
with beer for me and beer for you
and two more beers for two
then another beerbeer too
one more for me one more for you
yeah
one more

19. LITTLE HIGH

beautiful
the way you look
the way you look at things
so beautiful

the way you laugh
the way you talk
it's really great

your teeth
so white
your nose
so pretty
your words
that voice
that talk
your thing

so cute
so sweet
so sexy
what do I know

your sex
your breasts
your arse
all of that
your eyes

your light
your thoughts so

so big
your breadth
your yes
and your no
my longing
my will
my need
your desire

come on let's get out of here
now

quick let's go
to you
outta here
away from here
with you
to me
with me
to you to you

ACT ONE

'mmm hm, hm hmm,
if I could melt you heart'
– Madonna

I: In Bed

1. CONCEPTION

yes
yes
yes
yes
yes

yes yesyes

yes
yes
yes
yes
yes
yes
yeeeeees
God
that's good

yeah
so good
that's soooo good

2. I LOVE YOU

d'you think we could lie to each other already?
what do you mean lie?
if we had to lie now
if the wrong question came up?

what question?
could you lie to me
right now?
but why, what for?
even though we've only just – ?
come on, babe
I need to know
look, I'll show you

3. BEAUTY

they shag
they fuck
they do it
they get it on

what was that you just said?
they shag and fuck
they do it
they laugh?
oh right yeah

they do it to each other
and she does it to herself
and she does it to him
and they come together like mad

they hang on to each other

cuddling and stuff
they talk
they have a heart to heart
they talk and talk
and then do it again
and again and again

they shag
they fuck
they scream
and laugh

the doorbell rings

they stop
they wait
they listen
they whisper

I love you
I love you too
and they laugh
they fuck
and they kiss each other

Lover
Love
the doorbell rings
they stop

the doorbell rings really loud

Hey!
Twat!
we'll fuck as loud
as we want
tosser!

they shout
and let rip
and make love over
and over and over again
like maniacs

they talk
and hold
each other
tight
tell each other
things from the past
from tonight

Stories
things they've told

things they've hoped
things they've dreamed

thing's they've done
things they've thought
things they've said
the usual things

they're so close
like before when they –
they talk, they speak
they're aware that they're strangers

they look at each other
they hold each other tight
hard at each other
close to each other
now inside each other

God that's good

they're doing something amazing
something completely new
they're doing it now
they're doing it again

they're fucking
they're shagging
they're doing it
they're laughing

they're so tired now
they can hardly move
they're sore all over
almost all over
aren't they?

they do it
they breathe
they hold each other

they call it love
they sing with joy

4. OLD SONG

bruised lips
in the morning
and spots
red marks
all over my face
fresh wind
brilliant clouds
in the sky
racing by

been wanting
to go to bed with you
for ages now

I didn't know her at all
pretty cool
for an opening line

you're laughing
you look beautiful
with your hair roughed up

there's a trainer on the floor
silver
winking up at me

shall we go?
where?
dunno
come on quick
let's just go

then at the hotel
in the room
the cigarettes
forgotten of course
left them on the table
I nip and get some
and matches?
I pop back down

get some matches
we talk

so good
we touch
straight into a kiss
we're already falling
out of the chair
fantastic
we lie on the floor
we lie in bed

beautiful
incredibly beautiful
what every part of you
feels like
the things you do
the way you are
your body
and what's inside
beautiful

we shout
and are totally happy
we laugh then ask each other why

we're both wet
all over
everything's soaking
faces crotches
hair
the pleasure of doing it
all night long
incredible
incredibly good

in love with each other
immediately of course
watch out
don't say anything about that now
be careful

in the dawn then
other faces
lights out
and it fades in
the day arrives in fragments

I have a shower
you're still in bed
lying on your tummy
alone now
dash out
and fetch the papers
at the gateway to heaven
where?

that I love you

passionate and glowing
I return
you're standing there
dressed again
a woman
and a man
man and woman: beautiful

saying goodbye
in the lift going down
sex and laughter
a feeling as big as the whole world, course
hug and parting
that's good too
nice
both on our own now

bruised lips
in the morning
and spots
red marks
on my face
the wind

carrying lovers' messages
and new ideas of course
everything

we look up
clouds racing
we want
we will
we can
we should

something's gonna happen

I'm full of
I don't know
today maybe

5. THEY SMOKE

story of fear
tale of hatred
description of a scene of jealousy

'cos I love you
'cos I'm afraid of you
'cos I'm yours

conversation about everything
words of gentleness
very simple sentences

'cos you're here
'cos I can feel you
'cos we're us

beginning of something in close-up
and with enduring hope
we smoke and talk and
let ourselves be carried
from one thing to another

because we
I don't know
it seems to work anyway

by saying and speaking
by hinting and feeling
with an arm round the shoulder
with riches and beauty

because you
and because I
because together we

words
lips
eyes
forehead

because I love you love
because I can see you
lover
healing and sharing
creating and succeeding
happening and witnessing
loving and telling

because you me
and I you
because we both

and smoke and talk

6. THEY TALK

Parents come back. What are their faces like? My
mother's voice sounds just like a happy childhood. Tell
me again. What was it like? I remember the tranquility,
the normality and seriousness, the wonderful way one
day would pass quite regularly into the next, it was
delightful, unlike any other family I ever saw. There was a
steady, unspectacular interest in everyone, and a joy in
everything we experienced or could recount. Fears and

great thoughts, terrified faces and ghosts in the night: shh sshhhh. It's alright, it's alright. I didn't know I was the panicky one, that I was the one who was ill. I took my mother's advice and could see the message in her kind gestures, the understanding and melancholy in her eyes. I could see her wisdom, her beauty and that's how I was, I became her face.

Father was obsessed with productivity. Rushing around always looking for others doing the same. No social skills, fanatical about pronunciation, scared of intimate conversations the whole time, and prone to a high-pitched madness about the tiniest little detail, NO NO NO NO NO before every first word, several times a sentence. Mocking and cursing everything and everybody, non-stop. Restless, driven, forever in a hurry. A destroyer. A gentle man. A wild one. Of course he was loved, I loved him intensely and then of course, later on, I hated him just as intensely. Father's face reminds me of the difficult years of my anguished youth, a youth which wasn't youth. He's what makes my days now so precious.

7. THE DAWN

dark blue: most beautiful colour in the world
morning bells ring
who are they greeting?
who are they calling?
little sister sends a message

each feather
I find
every
old
crooked stone
each thread, scrap of material
bit of branch
every leaf, stalk
the remains of an old flower

everything not seen or thought of
shall be king or queen
in its own tattered universe

sought in haste
found with difficulty
woken in panic
a whole life long
so wild and winning
stubborn, uninhibited
beyond all proportion, so unyielding

in the end we did succeed in a lot of things
though mostly not most of them
and gifted
those who'd stayed behind
those who'd not yet left
with suffering and death
with pain and guilt
and knowledge and darkness
its power and its gentleness

every little flower, sister, 's yours
a smile from you
in our lives
every pigeon feather
the wind brings
comes as consolation
from little sister

8. AWOKEN

apple of my eye
my sweetheart
my blossom

my pet my love
you tickling under my arm
the smell of you

your skin
licked all over
my hard and soft
my stomach
spayed white and wet

my crotch
so good
my sweet
and everything

my you
and my me
my all for you

my sweetheart apple of my eye
my blossom

9. THEY SLEEP TOGETHER

and I saw
a new world born
briefly
in the child's eyes

then it was gone
everything was hard
everything hurt
no-one knew
why

I became cheeky
and high-spirited
mean and deceitful
now I was angry
I already knew how to swim

then in the evenings shame
praying in bed
the psalms
guilt
and the strictness of belief

RAINALD GOETZ

size
of space
on wheels
is it all going
open world

friendly brothers
arguing, fighting
territory, every man for himself
then later they talk
one always starts

not a single day at school
that wasn't a pleasure
learning to learn
sorry but
I enjoyed it
being given knowledge

being told things
by strangers all the time
and seeing strangers too
really close
every day

friendships
friends
boys, boys, boys
the reasons for affection
and tender feelings
given so far
aren't the only ones

I know

to be loved
unconditionally, it's normal
and more than that
to arouse a passion
in a friend you admire
we'll walk in hand in hand
secretly

now it can begin
everything's ready
come on

Outside

'the view in a beautiful place, friend, friend, friend'
– Brecht

II: Enter
The Homeless
From Goerlitz Station

[1. IN FRONT OF THE PALETTE

what are they doing here?
what?
them
I dunno
they want to come in here
bollocks
they do, look

2. ENTER THE HOMELESS FROM GOERLITZ STATION

piss off
you scum
let me through here
you cunt
you want a smack?
sorry, what?
'cos you're gonna get one
what

he does him in
he beats him up
he kicks the shit out of him
he screams and whimpers

hold it
hold on
you keep out of it

you sodding monkey
you wog, you worm, you piece of shit
you scum, you cunt
you fucking bastard arsehole stupid

try it
hey you
you just try it
you
come here
come on over here
you fuckhead
gonna fucking flatten you
no bother

3. ON THE GROUND

Lying on the ground there's a shopping list, handwritten, prolestyle. It's got words on it: written in sleep, by a grave, at a wake. Potatoes, eggs, cheese, meat. Afraid, arm, slave, hat. Stink, brutal, drunk, mental. Destroyed, broken, family, cupboard. Ledge, loss, let off, old. Dirty, cold, runny nose. Trying, shiver, hurry, worry. Scarf, wanted, bread, his leg.

What's that
there on the ground?

It's a shopping list.

Next to it? Lie the broken.
People, objects, desires.
Destiny, debts and dogshit.
Hasn't he already said that?
And that? What do you call that?
More dogshit. Isn't it?

dead bloke
yeah, some dead bloke

ah

no, just drunk. Yeah. A junkie, a dosser, course, a punk
and his dog. 'S alright then. Let's sit ourselves down.
Good idea.

4. CALL TO ARMS

ye broken of this earth
stand up
arise
we have here something
to drink

what's he say?

they're handing out
drinks

'bout time
let's go over
get us some wine

don't want any
wine today
today I'm gonna take heroin
well
that's not such a bad idea

5. FROM BELOW

Does the universe have a purpose?
When viewed from hell?
hard to say, what do you think?
I thought hell was a regular part of it,
the so called universe,
where we are practically.

You mean the universe
is suffering and torture?

Nah, why, 's bollocks.
We don't just suffer,
we get on pretty well,

keep out of each other's way,
don't you reckon?
Perspective depends doesn't it?
Though, I dunno, well, yes,
what do you call it? Never mind, give us
the bottle, and have a swig
yourself first.

You going swimming?
No, going for a kip.

6. RED GREY

Who are you?
It's me.
Don't think so.
Hang on.
That was too quick for me.

Then the other one comes up, she says
she's too rough.
Are you? Does that hurt?
She says she didn't say nothing, she was just talking
she's nothing to say here.
I don't understand, says he, why, and she goes
that figures.
Then everything changes
she decides she'll teach him,
reach him outside and in
under his thin skin. Ah, aha, I see, says he, and she,
she doesn't give in. To him.
No way.

Language, she tamed it, she took it, she made it her own.
She told it it was her life and she was the one doing the
talking.
She walked, she ran, she wasn't too steady,
she spilt things, she drank, him too.
Go on, neck it, she went, he stood there silent
in the face of her words, missing in action.

He grabs the girl
she's eleven now,
he likes that,
he's got a finger.

He thought he loved her
she feels herself being touched
they're alone now,
there's something about her.

That's nice.
Do you like me?
And how, darling,
now
open your legs
and I'll take a closer look.

Oh wow
great.]

7. HAPPINESS

the rhythm, the message, the colour, the funk
the music, the city, the sound of words
the concept, the art, destruction of time
the echo, the dark, the mean and the dirty
the true and the real, the real and the slow
the fuckers, the suckers, the dick and the pussy
the sex and the flesh, the kiss and the ass
the clean and the true, the truth and the lie
the open and closed, the end and another
begin of beginnings, the death and the dark
the heavy, the slow, the lower, the higher
the better, the last, the rhythm, the messages
the colour, the funk, the music of word,
the word of the words, the music of time
of time, time, time, of time, time, time
time, time, time
time

course, I know
what you mean

he takes her by the hand
and leads her away
hands round her neck
he's taken her clothes
she's so warm
then she turns blue
he's
she can't
now he wakes the dogs
it purifies her
kind of brutal
yeah
but it happens

8. THE GOOD LORD

he reckons yeah
he invented all this
he made it
he was the inventor
responsible
he'd put his hand up
he'd just ask
everyone
to listen for a moment
only doesn't seem to be
all that interesting
he thinks now
hey, listen to this
I invented all of this here

you serious?

yeah
for instance
this was a while ago
he'd invented a couple
did they not know that?

benefit, too, was his idea
even Mercedes, and BMWs
he'd made all the MPs
the stock exchange and money and stuff
yeah honest
they might laugh
but it was true
it had really taken it out of him
all this
all those years, you know
he'd even invented beer
cigarettes and the colour green
and the political party to go with it
elections and all that
everything there is here
invented, thought up in his head
now he asks again
what they think of that
the burdens he carries
inside
him

mm, hmm

now they were silent
course they wouldn't believe him
ok
he could see that
but they'd be wrong
he said out loud
you're wrong
take laws for example all of them
who did them, yeah: him, he invented them
he was knackered, well, how could anyone stand it
they'd just end up laughing
at him, that would be a mistake
they'd see
they'd understand
eventually

even him, people like him
and him, and that one over there, yep
the others too he'd made all of them
him, for instance, yeah, him

aha

[he steals his jacket
he nicks his money
he pinches his gear
I'll have that
now he laughs at him
and fucks off
he's robbed him
who was supposed to be the Lord here
of the tramps and the rentboys
the beggars and the liars
ambassadors of the underclass
that fits
he reckoned, yeah, that's
how he planned it, wiser
than God himself

aha, aha
giz a fag
giz a light

watch it you
oi oi oiii

he decks him
he beats the living crap out of him
he kills him quick
he croaks and dies]

9. THE NIGHT

so they sat there, yeah there, that's right
so they sat there drinking
drinking beer and drinking wine.
They had some smokes and smoked them,

they talked and smoked cigarettes,
had a bit of draw as well,
they drank vodka, they took a bit of
cocaine, then heroin, they sat there
and felt pretty good.
They were about half caned by now.
A copper came, decent bloke,
they had to move on, alright?
Alright, mate, don't worry,
no fuss, no bother, no trouble.
They moved on, round the corner,
sat down on a nice wall.
They sat there and talked.
They saw people coming out of the opera.
Evening sir have you got any spare change?
They saw people coming out of the club,
out of the theatre and they said,
poor fuckers, going to the theatre
get your money out,
we need new drugs it's an emergency.
They were given fresh cash
and in exchange they gave their misery,
to boost the mood
of the rich and better off.
They bought food,
they'd felt hungry suddenly,
bought vodka, a bit of wine,
a tiny bit of heroin, and more cocaine.
They had more drugs,
more draw, a drink, they felt ok.
It wasn't so cold that night,
it was summer, a good time,
they sat there and talked.
They talked and talked, look,
said one. Where? There. Oh him. Right.
What's that?
That's got to be an artist.
I can tell, one look,

that's an artist,
it's obvious,
I can tell.
An artist, fuck me,
Jesus, an artist.
What kind of life
can that be?

ACT TWO

'it had the aura
of a heroic and polemically
creative place'
– Richard Meier

II: The Firm

1. IN BED

Babe?
yes?
I love you
I love you too, babe
shall we
you bet

2. IN THE STUDIO

scuse me?
yeah?
am I too early?
what?
the woman from Vogue
's on the phone

is she mad?
what time is it?
just coming up to eleven
tell her to call back later
the cow
certainly
and please could you
bring some breakfast
of course
and the newspapers

and so on
sure

FUCKINGHELL

was there anything else?
nono
only joking
you're not in a bad mood
are you?
I'm in a brilliant mood
what else could I be in
that's great
I think so too
I'm glad
me too

3. THIS MORNING

she brings breakfast
a golden start to the day
magnificent, new, light
he leaps out of bed
a huge space
the morning sun smiles
he smiles

what was that you said
it was so true just now?

he's got the newspaper in his hand
he waves the paper
he sits
down
reads, starts swearing
makes sweeping gestures, hand signals
scratches his head for a moment
scratches his neck
he's suddenly excited
wait, he's got an idea, an idea?
where from, how, why? wait a minute

I think
I've just got
an idea

what kind of thing was it?
this idea?
where did it come from?
and who made it?
and above all
how did they make it?
he laughs for a moment, he
touches his head again
stands up, paces up and down
and laughs and is happy
it seems, it's obvious

er, er
this is great
this is yeah
yeah

he grabs some paper
you can see him scribbling
a question:
what is the artist noting there?
you can see the silk of his dressing gown
the damp gleam of porcelain
the shimmering decanters
you can see his haste, see the hunger
with which the artist drinks, coffee, orange juice
he puts down the cup, how did that go again?
he'd just, now looks up
into the air, he appears to see something up there
he goes to the window, laughs
and greets the outside world
greets the tree, shouts out

I've got it
I've got it yeah
yeah

he dashes back to his papers
mumbles something like get it down, get it down
he does, he does, thinks about Kleist
he needs more light, time, time
he feels good now, yes
he sees himself in a world
that's now, how can you say it?
he laughs, he shrugs, a good sign

yeahyeah
yeah

we want artists to be or become
happy, don't we?
want them to be able
to recognize, perceive and welcome
everything, even terrible things
in that state, so that from there, with that, they can

nah nah
no no
erm hmm
he seems to have made a mistake
somehow taken a wrong turning
anger rises
what now?
in the artist's body
where to where from exactly?
not to recognize, no
he shakes himself
he's
got it
seems to smile, seems to grin
this way or that way, or maybe even like this?
he seems to be deliberating
seems to be rejecting something
he clearly enjoys it
in a way

yeah yeah
yeah yeah

he drinks more coffee, drinks juice
he laughs, he's happy, goes to the window
stands there without speaking, looks out and nods
the artist's full of the need to act
he's happy with his life
can see the form of the new work in front of him
a new object, which he already is
that just quickly has to be made visible
to the rest of the world through him
what do you mean: has to
he wants it to, he thinks it'll be cool
for other people and for him, you can see that now
you can see him thinking that

cool cool cool
that is cool
that's exactly how it's gotta be done

[4. IN THE STUDIO

A paper on staging conflict. Comments on the paper.
Discussion of the comments. There's an anger in the
room, unspoken, between the people there, there in the
emptiness. At the times when things could be said,
nothing is. People turn away, pretend to be busy, exude
coldness through silence. It works, anger builds. Silence
prevails. For how long then? Only very briefly, silence
can't be any more than a single moment of non-verbality,
a pause and freeze. The silence stands there, paralysed,
briefly, very briefly, almost super-briefly. The next moment
begins. The artist is standing in the space. His staff say
nothing. They're silent. And the artist asks, what's up,
what's going on? That's too much for the staff suddenly,
that was uncalled for, that was not on, now it all goes
off.

Outrage
anger
in the sense of –

punish
leave
really care
she would, whereas he
contract, lawyers, courtroom, backside
you'll see, he will, he will see, he'll

The artist is amazed, he's practically open-mouthed. Ok so he's got. Payment, position, ambition. His comments. Requiring improvements, demanding corrections. Can we now look at it as, can we say, that's right, that's not right. He retracts those comments, he. He can appreciate that, he'll get that sorted out. Maybe he didn't quite to the extent required, ok, he'll. He asks for, he doesn't know what. The staff look angry. The artist realises he can't do this, it's just not him. This isn't about money, it's not about power, not about ideas. It's about maturity and the lack of it. The artist is simply too infantile to be able to manage perfectly simple things. A perfectly normal argument for example. This annoys people, his avoiding them, the fact that he doesn't understand how to use meaningless words, just to reassure people that everything's ok, it's fine, it's alright. He annoys people with his absurd precision. From an abstract perspective this is entirely reasonable but from a human one it's a complete disaster. The artist appreciates this. But he can't stop himself. He's now planning something which could solve all this, maybe, if it works, in an artistic form of course, obviously, he's planning what he calls his child complex.]

5. CONCEPT

the artist is now sitting in his office
the day's going well, the files arrive
his assistant brings coffee, his secretary
looks cute, it's ok, it's alright, he can't complain
there's a phone call, what's this about Bild, he says
I'm not talking to Bild

and sends for his paid underartist
explains new designs to him, new desires, ideas
the idea, for example, he had this morning
the underartist nods
he approaches, he laughs, agrees
has a point, hesitates
and makes it

[good point
right
I'd forgotten that
seems to finally show all those ambitions
all that suffering in a different light
why get away from that, I feel that's kind of
seems to me]

the question is
how's it gonna work?
does it work?
how?
the underartist is trying

[I thought the main thing was the intention,
the new plan
making more precise this idea of a somehow
diffuse, but I dunno, nevertheless
yeah, sorry, I really do
think, the idea is

the underartist watches sternly
and his artist begins to falter]

I see
yes yes
anyway

the conversation fizzles out, you've got to say,
into abstraction, it remains pretty abstract
it really hasn't got very definite so far
what has been definite this morning
like I said, was the row with the technicians
about very pressing deadlines,

about those seven enormous pictures
the five massive sculptures,
brand new and ready the day before yesterday, waiting for
the people from the shippers
there's also the guest list, for the party tomorrow
after the big event, the opening
of the new Hetzler Gallery
in its new space,
in the city centre, top location, yeah
so everything needs doing and it's all got to be done at
once
like always basically and
right now
there's this young man
who's just come in
said hello very politely, introduced himself, sat down,
starts, begins, it's for the big interview
the artist finally wants to give everything away, say
everything
reveal himself to everyone, how he is, how he sees
himself
his thing and his work, he wants to spell it out finally
to the world, once and for all
[he's made time for that today
he feels today, he's got to say, he says
sorry a bit erm –

exactly
how can you put it?
chaotic, maybe a bit chaotic
yeah, chaotic
that's it chaotic
I've got this enormous longing for
a real clarity in myself
I can sense things that, I don't know
shall we begin? are we starting now?
by all means, thank you, now we can]
are you recording this?

6. THE INTERVIEW

I
then
until
yeah right

aha
aha aha
haha haha

after that
by contrast
for our
absolutely

mmm
hmm

they're gonna
we can
has to be done
we're

if you want to put it that way
definitely no question at all

I use
I gave
I had
till yesterday

but now
does this mean?

hard to say
taking shape
very good
and soon

sounds exciting

but without
resisted

though mostly
that's his name

all this since yesterday?

yeah since then
concepts
she can almost
she'll never

aha and
right yeah

I've got to say
admit
refused
thanks
very much
I've

no but
get together
we ought to
you've got

tomorrow night

definitely

7. DREAM

That's no good. No, sorry. It's useless. The whole thing's
a load of shite. You can't, I mean nobody wants, who is
going to, how could she? Yeah, no really, no no, definitely
not. The artist hits the back of his head. His brain
flashes, an image is produced, right in the cortex opticus.
A reflex carries the brain forward where it collides with the
frontal lobes deep inside the skull. An act of will also
results from this minor trauma, it shoots round his entire
head, briefly stimulating the whole brain. Only what was
that exactly? What kind of image was it? What did this
will just now want? The image before, or after? The artist

searches inside himself and can't find anything, he feels
his previous thought again, everything I do is useless, a
mistake, what's going on here, bollocks, fucked, past it.
It's wrong, it's never going to go anywhere, doubt
becomes despair, despair turns into anger, and anger
gives way to tiredness, exhaustion, hatred. That's it. His
stupid head sinks down into his hands. The artist thinks
he could scream, he sighs irritated and says nothing.
Then something suddenly evaporates and out of that
silence within the artist something beautiful emerges:
sleep.

inside him now
the deities appear
in this precise moment
and they see
what they see there
they see the one they love
tolerate
perfectly ordinary
and nod gently
and say
a little more
a little bit more
yes

8. OPEN GARDEN

Then his wife and consort entered the room, saw her
lover lying there at odds with himself, with his work and
with the world. She walked up closer to him till she was
standing behind him and looked down on his face. He
made her happy, he was hers and she was his somehow.
She opens her arms, presses her stomach against him
from behind and lowers her head against his, letting him
feel her sex in his dreams. She doesn't know the precise
details, she just offers him what she can feel in herself,
an indistinct form, aged, arrived from somewhere else
perhaps, some distant time and place in space,
somewhere in motion rather than fixed, something elusive

rather than a precise and definite point. He jumps up. He's woken up. He turns round, she smiles and he laughs. Faces happy to see each other. He's the man who belongs to her, and she's the woman who somehow makes all his efforts – well she gives them meaning, allows him to learn from them, understand them, through love. They want to celebrate this, that this is how it is, for her, for him, they give themselves to each other, they kiss, they do it, they make love, they achive nakedness, conception, pregnancy, birth. In this way to the artist a son and to his wife, who he makes a mother, a child is born. Something has happened here which happens relatively often on the earth. They're together now, they're staying together, they're parents together and they're looking into their child's face, as it cries, this new life, crying. For what?

9. MEALTIME

round the table the talk is
of other people, co-workers
predecessors and friends
allies and rivals
of what's been read, seen and thought up
the son's there
he laughs
the son's full of questions
questions that are new to the artist
he's pleased with the child's questions
he sees the child as an asset
he's mistaken there
he's mistaken a lot of the time actually
he bangs on the table
the son is startled
the artist doesn't like
children annoying him, he likes quiet children
who are clever, educated, cautious and sensitive
that's how he sees his son, like him aged five
grown up, ready, complete
exactly the person he is today

the son has long since stopped crying
he looks straight at them and asks about new names
then everything is discussed in detail
without fuss, pleasantly, in detail

[10. CONTRADICTION

Hang on. He sits. He paces. It's ok. He stands still.
She comes, she's expected, and sees. She sees.
It's ok, she writes, they are, he says.
Portrait. The slit. She laughs. The bloom.
He says. She comes. Why? I'd do the same for them.
She sits and laughs. He stands, she goes.

11. CONCENTRATION

A contradiction of materials. Doubt in rustproof steel.
Love out of wood. Fear in porcelain. A thought as a
photo. An ideal as a painting. Contingencies carved.
Goodness out of ice. Money out of plaster. Trust as a
metaphor. Plants and flowers, little tiny arses. Meaning
as a basic concept. Sociology. A plan as carpet. Intention
as mosaic. Revolution in marble. Beauty abstract.
Shadows black and white. Reflex of one colour.
Contingent contrast. Figures in need. Reversable walls.
White as the sphere. Wishes in old. Mood out of pixels.
Word perfect.

12. AND BEFORE AND BEFORE THAT AND

a point, a line, I can see you talking
a big space, you, with room
and all these, your, ah
aha, I see, good that's nice
she laughs
the others, the round, your blue
in the gentle tug of grieving eyes
there are lots there already
movement everywhere
we have a look round ourselves now, heaving

we breathe in and talk
we eat something and turn away
we touch things and quickly phone somebody
we're not understood, what, what
we try again
we're shouting now
now someone comes over
they look nice and laugh
we say something to them
and they just laugh and nod
we start shouting again
the lights go out
this is impossible

I'm frightened
I defend myself
I know how
I'm developing
I'm looking forward to tomorrow
only one thing: I'm not playing
I'm happy to watch

we run together
we sing in chorus
we talk a hell of a lot
we like each other straight away
we argue a lot too
don't you?

offered and given
stretched, dazed
disarmed and blessed
hoped for then lost
we both thought
it would be really good
we're coming from theirs
might as well go along
out of friendship
and outside

spontaneously
before the end
they said they wanted to
which was great, course
so did we]

13. WORK

the mood is right
the artist
walks through his studios
he talks to his people
he praises them, says things are wonderful
expects corrections here and there

vision, idea, concept, paper
form, power, conquering
resistance, the opposite wall
breakthroughs, action, recognition, deed
back, not like that, no. Like this

yeah, yeah,
keep still, like this
yeah, that's it
now try it again, yeah, got it

we could make this bit here
a bit lighter I think, and there
bigger, brighter, warmer maybe

I see, that makes sense
it's quite clear, it's obvious
explaining, talking, looking
at the others looking and
gesturing to indicate what he means

the objective here or the intention is
the same as always
perfection and completeness
to render the manufacturing process invisible
while retaining a clue to its genesis

the ultimate degree
of mastering a skill
says a blue coated workman says
to his apprentice
is when no trace of it remains

and one of them mixes the paint
it's a bright pink
and a vibrant yellow
it's for a flowering twig
and one of them always talks a bit too much
and the other one would rather keep his mouth
shut and daydream
while he's painting, totally focused
one makes an animal out of plaster
it's got a hat on its head
like coincidentally the guy on the steel
elephant, who measures and cuts
saws, fits, trims and
separates and stands back
he checks the effect
does the effect work?
the way it was originally supposed to?
is it different now?
how? how come? is it
really better, lighter, more spherical?
what was the plan, hang on,
wait, wait a minute, he
calls for the boss, hey boss
could you come over here, we need
to talk about the effect here,
quick, please, yeah, it's urgent

the boss comes over
he's standing next to another painter
who's also busy painting a picture
a different picture
also made with colours
of course, that's obvious, what else could it be made with

RAINALD GOETZ

with canvas and oil, with coloured pigments
which are mixed and applied to this so called wall
of canvas, according to a previously
determined plan, determined by the artist
according to the idea which is occupying him at the
moment
what's occupying him right now
is the early world
the time of spectacle, of amazement and of touch
the time of fear and worry
soothing and comforting
the time when words could sound magical
when calm occurs inside someone, if someone
calmly says calm,
calm down, be calm, nice and calm, yes, calm

[yes, that's what these pictures are about
it's very pleasant
you've got to say
pleasant
the pictures also work through their form
through size and its opposite, reflecting potential
in the sense of an insight
into ancient wisdom, undisturbed,
removed so to say, cleared away
deleted, swept off, fixed
without being hidden in some stupid way
no tricks or secrets
it's about viewing things
from a universal perspective
about what everyone knows
and carries inside them somehow,
it's about people's dreams, which are revealed, singly,
in each picture, one by one, contemporary, yes,
you could say, critical, alright
don't talk it to death
ok, Jesus, I'm never going to say it again
something'll have been gained then

won't it? eh?
through this new vow of silence?
it expresses the awkwardness better
that viewers have looking at the pictures
everyone has something to do, unconnected
with the pictures here
organizing their lives
nothing to do with art
wanting to show that aspect too
that's one of these pictures' many broader objectives
non-art, the everyday, inconspicuousness, very gently
all impossible of course, yeah, obviously, doesn't matter
it's going in the right direction, you can see that,
heading the right way, definitely

the boss now goes over to his co-worker, he sees
it's good, it works, it's fine like that
the way we planned it and they talk about
what happens next, right, the
boss is in a good mood
the day is going well
things are coming, growing, becoming
he nods, he reads something quietly
he's reading something he's interested in
there's something about a stone cultivator
who creates garden rocks
in genuine and bizarre natural formations
using tides and diverted streams
that's what it says, the artist nods, he breathes in and out
he sighs, a bit too much art here
he thinks to himself and says, I've got to get out of here,
now,
right out of here, right now, get out, yeah, just out]

14. FRESH AIR

he opens the window
air pours in
the birds are calling really loud

the trees are rustling
maybe
spring's on its way
and everything starting afresh

I've
I did it
I've done it
I washed it in water
I sprayed it
had another look at it
I tried this
I think it still needs
I've still got to I've not finished

he opens the window
summer
grass
he can feel the
heat
he's panting
he runs

got to get out there
in the wilderness
go looking for it
my skin hurts all over
I'm sick I want to hide
and seek
and curl in deep
up in a big red

he opens the window
he can smell the fruit
gleaming
in the afternoon light
leans into the daylight
and he nods

he can see a boy
a child
good looking
he can feel a beauty
inside him coming from there
he longs
for something
he feels
no longer sick
he sees there
watching and he sees
that it's good
that nothing's doing any harm
he waits and shakes
a little, nothing bad
it's ok, he's fine
he can't and he doesn't want to
he can't complain

he opens the window
seeds circle all over the place
so early
Father?
Can I still
I have to, I need to
oh
ohhhh
he takes a deep breath
and breathes it out again
it's out
it's nice out
but out's out now

[15. WOODCUT

He sits there drinking. He's come from outside. He talks.
He's silent. I'm poor. I'm ill. I'm hungry. I'm going to be
sick. I stink and smoke and spit and puke. I shout and
growl, I'm made up. I hate all of you. I think I'm great. I
drink and stink, and I spit on you. I'm a criminal, a

granny, a student. I work for the council. I'm joining the army. I've come straight from home. I'm moving on. I'm stopping here. I'm looking for a place. I'm gonna have a kip. I'll get up afterwards. I'll just have a drop. I'll be right there. I used to be a copper. I'm in the church now. I'll go along later. I'm fucked off with this anyway. I pray to God. If it helps, it helps. I snore. I couldn't give a toss. I sleep in the open. I can fly. I can think. I talk when I'm speaking. And drink what I can. There are times I've got to throw up. I wash my mouth. I comb my beard. And sing and move. I kneel. I shout. I'm alive. I'm going to my grave. I sit on a bench. I listen to music. I play the violin. I play the piano. I play records. I cross myself. I can hear ringing. I hate bells. I'm afraid. I'll go in now. I'll just come for a bit. I'll just nip up there. I'll take a look over there. I read words. Understand what they mean. Couldn't agree more. I'm happy for you. I'm not very tired. I yawn and burp. I scratch my knee. My bum itches. My fingers have sores on. Lips are fucked. I take a quick look at him. I look away again. I say something soft. I say enjoy. I say love. Say things I said before. Long time ago now, childhood. I'm my mother. The barman comes round. I'm closing now. I'll have another beer. I drink and smoke. I pop to the loo. I stink and wave. My cock's hanging off me. I'm dripping. There's a knock. The door opens. I look out of the window. I'm sitting by the river. I'm thrashing in the water. I can't get any air. I swallow some of it. Anybody can drown. I hang myself. I lie down in the grass. I take pills. I jump off the roof. I set fire to myself. I cut myself open. I'm pissed off. I shout at you. I kick and scream. I whisper a lot. I know someone there. I've heard. Forgotten now. That reminds me. I was going to. Grape, I think. Wine and beer. I'm all at sea. Covered in a pile of. I think we have. We want to be dignified. I'm drinking and sinking. I'm sinking back. I'm sinking the way I sing. More of a growl. I'm lying on my back. I'm lying on my stomach. I'm not drunk. I'm just light-headed. I get light-headed and listen and get things mixed up. I've got two ears, two eyes and a mouth. I walk on legs. Here are my hands. I hold on to the bottle. I'm good at things. I've got hair. I'll head over there. I look up. It's raining. It's drizzling. I think that was it. That's it, here. I'll manage. I think we should go. I reckon this is it. I'll say cheers. I'll give you a shout, see you. I'm laughing, a puddle. I'm lying in the dirt. I sleep and breathe. I don't notice anything. The wind's blowing. There's thunder. There's lightning. He lies there sleeping. He lies there in the open. He looks pretty good.]

16. SCULPTURE

ok
ok
ok
ok

wait
it's stuck
it's just got stuck

alright
I'll wait
hang on
what's going on?

just a moment
moment longer
it's still stuck

and now?
what's happening?
what's going on?

it's stuck
it's still stuck

now
now it's ok

is it ok?

it's ok
ok
ok
ok

is everything alright?

yeah yeah
fine
ok

good
it's good to hear that

yeah
you know
ok
ok

you think
that's ok?

I think so
I mean
that was what I
that's ok

that's ok
so we can
let's get it
it's ok like that

cool
awesome
excellent
just blows me away

my first
wow, hey, gorgeous
thank you, right, I think
that's enough, that's it

ok
ok
ok
ok

fine
ok, fine
absolutely
ok

I'm really thrilled
going to stay like that, leave it
it's finished, yeah
it's right like that, right

that's this sculpture here
a rough representation
and it shows it
in the moment
he sees it, in that moment
there's something hanging from one hand
a piece of paper, looks like it's got writing on it
the usual symbols, creating meaning out of words
and vision out of meaning
illuminating, there's really
no other way to describe these things
fully illuminating their meanings, text
in other words, there's a bit of text hanging there
yes there is, and it's the sketch, yes
it really is the sketch hanging
from one hand
and fluttering in the wind

17. SKETCH

Art
a weekend of art
the club
and the studio
the gallery and the homeless

the homeless from Goerlitz Station
on the march
a play
in seven acts
all neatly packaged

you said
it's about love
you said
it's about art
it's about talking
pictures, tunes
it's about argument
and agreement
it's about people
who've got something to say, to do
whatever
it's about creation and giving birth
about things, objects
and ideas
it's about the everyday
truth and banality
it's not really about narrative
not a lot gets decided here
there's not much shouting
it's about concern
and melancholy
it's about rhythms
like some music
about hearing
a long way off
it's generally about general things
what you could call the language of our times
it's about mistakes
perfection
that's too neat
it's not rough enough
not wild enough

and nowhere near
excessive
enough

it's about a moment
which exists
in people's lives too
at least briefly
sometimes it does
it's
this might sound stupid
about harmony
that's not true
no, stop, that's wrong, bollocks
it's the opposite
it's about never finding harmony

After the Interval

IV: The Opening

1. OUTSIDE

what's it look like?
great
shall we go in then?
definitely

2. PREAMBLE

the curtain falls
the curtain has fallen
the curtain rises
and there's a pause
then the pause ends
the light goes out
the murmuring stops
the music fades
a moment's silence

now the curtain rises once again
and right in the light
an aah
Oooh
Eee
the new first scene
the opening

and it begins

[3. PRELUDE

once upon a time
in the days
there was once
at this time
many years ago
it's a long time ago
a brilliant artist
of such quality
that the king said
bring me this
artist
I want to see him
want to set him to work
ask
what he thinks and does
how he
sees the world
things like that
everyone
off you go
and get a move on
if I may say so
who knows
how much longer
I shall live
I want to talk to him
this artist
want to see him

and of course it happened
as the king had decreed
the artist
was brought there
he stood before his king
saluted him, bowed
and said
here I am
my king

as requested
it is an honour
I am yours
to command

you've got to picture the king now
as someone
who has contemplated and witnessed
all manner of things upon the earth
except the suffering
debts and shortages
he has himself increased
during his reign
which wasn't very good
most of the time
and what was on his mind
most was the burden
which he felt he –]

4. THE OPENING

Hang on a minute, wait. There's something else over
there, what was that? Oh, yeah, right, the opening.
Course. That's it. You're by the door going in, then you're
inside and then you end up by the door again. People
going in and people coming out again. Who's coming?
Who's going in? Good to see you. Yeah, it's nice to be
here. It's great you could come, what would you like to
drink. I'm going to wait thanks, I'm going to go inside.
You do that, enjoy it. Sure I will, thanks, thank you.

helllo
should've known
you too?

course, yeah

shit
fuck
terrific

,'t it
'm really pleased

yeah yeah, well
it's ok, what about you?

hello
helllo

very beautiful
I thought so too

then we
those ones
now they really
not where

why not
that's exactly it

exactly, exactly
exactly exactly exactly

Conversation. This critic's saying he thinks racism ought be banned. Ought to be what? They banned racism ages ago. Yeah, I know, but like more. And then other one goes: ban is such a great word. It sounds so cool, it feels like possibility and difference, like intervention, like let's stop fucking around talking, discussing arguments, ban sounds like: game over. It sounds, in left wing parlance, revolutionary. Only the question then becomes, whether it actually achieves anything, or if just provides comfort for those calling for the banning. Threatening to make opinions punishable, albeit as a diversion from focussing on behaviour, creating hate laws in the form of anti-hate laws, is only going to promote hatred and won't make the world any better, because the world just won't let itself be controlled that directly. You can't exclude evil, speech has to include it, discuss it, work it over backwards and forwards and then slowly, it's an incredibly slow process, you can change it, disarm it, make it harmless. If you

want to take it to an extreme, every evil sentence that
isn't an evil act is actually a good act because it begins to
integrate and weaken that evil. That's how he sees it,
that's how he thinks it operates, not the other way round,
well more that than the other way in any case. Etc etc.

[What? Oh yeah, the critics
who are talking there, the conversation
in that corner over there. They're arguing about this piece
that was in the paper recently.
The author's replying to his critics.
Conversation turns radical writing
into anecdote, it makes it questionable, softens it you
could say.
The new truths arising out of that
in the chaotic field of talk are further ammunition
and an additional burden, they're a few more
possibilities, realised in verbal form.
The more that gets written, the more gets said, so −

he on the other hand emphasised
that every attempt had to be made first
to reach a negotiated
solution

on the night before the election
a car bomb
went off in one of the suburbs
injuring four people

four wins
I'm convinced about that
power has been brought to bear

I hardly care
like here]

and I would say things like
this is Jane
and her father likes black men
and her mother had a facelift

and she's just the girl for you
because she'll boss you around
and you like that

wrong

ok, can I
try another one

sure

this is Tom
he's a chubby chaser

that's better

and if I can't remember two people's names
so I can't introduce them
I just do a big sigh and say
oh, I'm so tired of introducing people
I've been doing it all night
why don't you introduce yourselves

I think we were
introduced before
weren't we

yes, I, we
the thing
it's really great

cool
it's so out there
fucking hell
now this is really

exactly, course
exactly exactly

More conversation. Conversation about
the position of the artist.
About the book about the painter's studios,
not being able to photograph bunny
the cut-glass plinth for the bust of the artist,

and about heard and unheard prayers.
About favourite films of all time and the structure of
speech,
about the gallery owner's son and his jacket,
the new museum, old pictures
conversation about parties, receptions and labels,
about existence and the lack of lightness
in the discursive web here and not here,
there and elsewhere,
in them and in the others, in ourselves, and in
conversations
about books about reason in society.
Conversation between people from museums
and people who run galleries,
between buyers and young turks,
between curators, fans and genuine collectors,
between people who have money and people who haven't
any at all,
between the drop dead gorgeous and others who aren't
quite so pretty,
real players and liggers,
and also between loads of people the same as each
other,
between old and old, middle-aged and middle-aged,
that too. It's all here, in this room,
at this moment, because everybody's here.
[Words have come,
glances and envy,
admiration, some terrible feelings too,
perfectly normal ones, moments of nausea, of escape,
of a longing to be left alone for while,
then it's gone,
someone laughs,
producing laughter in someone else,
that gets picked up by the next person
then carried on
and so on and so on.

you haven't
got a light have you?

glass of white wine?
or a glass of water?
orange juice maybe?

may I?
thank you

of course
by all means

It's ok, thanks, I've already
you don't?

could we maybe outside
a gentle

I'm sorry I've only
got the other kind with me

A waitress walks round offering hors d'oeuvres
people look at the tray,
they look in the young woman's face,
the mood lifts, they drink and talk
and the question comes up
where the artist is now.
In an abstract form: what is the current position of the
artist?
He must be somewhere, that's obvious.
There, in the crowd, or maybe on the fringes,
maybe right in the middle, who knows.
The thing is his position is entirely free.
Not even the work determines the place
the artist occupies.
He can be working with film, with music,
he can place himself in a sociological, or literary context,
or in the tradition of the new, he can have abandoned
the artistic field altogether,
he will still return there

entirely as he wishes.
And with this freedom he
carries a final burden,
the position of the individual set against the whole,
that's what's great about this new position.
From there the focus now moves on to the pictures,
and from the pictures back on to us.

5. THE PICTURES

Man with red horse blanket
in front of the big pictures
big entrance
lights, glitter, sounds good

Man with thick felt hat
the man with a woman, the woman with a dog
the dog with a puppy and a mouse
the mouse with a little mouse and that's it for the mouse

a woman with a thing, the man with a hole,
a really erotic glass sculpture

then this marble thing, huge
oh, right, that's really coarse,
brutal, it's really cool

the flowers and the birds
the bees and the animals
oh God, wow,
that's cute, look, and carved out of wood
then painted bright colours

a pinky-reddish slice of cake
gigantic and real, a little baby
and more taste and cuteness
a policeman with a bear in a fairy tale world

it's good, it's good
he says nothing for a moment
it's really very nice]

what's happening?
what's going on here?

him over there
speech
quiet please
just one moment please

thank you thank you

6. THE SPEECH

Ladies and gentlemen, friends of our gallery, the art that you see here tonight, an art whose fear and suffering manifests itself in the paranoid form of perfection, whose image of dirt and corruption is one of cleanliness and asepsis, an art which seems to be practically trembling with panic, not to mention its insulated subjectivity in the deeply private world of its creator, while continually crying out all the louder to communicate, trying to cry out, thinking it must cry out, to be more precise, yes, the more hopelessly it sees itself captured inside the prison of its own autistic obsession, an art trying so desperately to be loved that it provokes, arouses, creates hatred, disgust, resistance, rejection and protest to such a degree that everything about it which aims to be perfectly simple, logical, direct, illuminating and on the most basic level attractive becomes absurd, grotesque, ridiculous, rubbish, which provokes such a mass of contradictions, all the more for its craving nothing more than peace and respect, attention and display, for comfort and reward: this art is political. And its politics, ladies and gentlemen, consist of fear. It is the voice of a traumatized child. Within the confines of this fear everything is big, very big, threatening, frightening and distorted into caricature. This fear searches desperately with wide open eyes for moments of non-badness, where things aren't all broken or destroyed. There, look. A chance to breathe, if only for a moment. That is the mechanism behind these pictures here. Measured against this, against the struggling energy that the solutions here are based on, the insistence of other artists on their ideas of malignity, whether it be the not unattractively fascinating pubertal art of Mike Kelly or the more mature, wailing grown-up horror of Croenenberg, continually demanding new and stronger kicks - just to name two examples - seems bourgeois, insensitive and underpowered. None of our sculptures here, none of these pictures simply affirms negativity, or even, on the other hand, affirms the positive. Here, too, this art is political, in that it doesn't devalue its own aspects of protest and affirmation to an ideal of a better life, however correct it may be, those struggles for a political ideal, however good, being accompanied by considerable gratification and social recognition, instead it reproduces the reality of life as it is genuinely lived, which is always both, approval and condemnation of injustice, of protest, of the demand that everything should be changed, immediately, and that very particular things should stop and finally show some real improvement on the way they are now, and not without ultimately including a positive desire, or at least not ignoring it at any rate, which motivates every single breath taken, life itself, that thirst, the desire to grab hold of the glass and drain it dry. And with those words, dear friends, I'd like to welcome you all here, wish you all a marvellous evening, and I'm very pleased to raise a glass with you all to the art we can see here, to the richness of its experienced contradictions, to what it so publicly hides. Cheers, Ladies and Gentlemen, your very good health, all of you.

[7. MORE TALK

you think he thinks
in other words, he did think

yeah sure course
why shouldn't he
at all
and whatsitcalled

I dunno
how can that
her who else
on the other hand
and somehow
but they can't only
no, prevent it

seems more
people want to get in
how are they going to do it?
it's so full

some people want to get out
others want to go in, what's so special

more hors d'oeuvres?
another bite?
vision of a moment
of warmth?
a friendly face?

a yes
a cheers
thank you
a no I've already
a yeah
a can I have another
take two
me too
very nice
charming
thank you
you're welcome
warmth
a fancy another one
top-up
repeat
and start all over again
thank you.]

8. COMMOTION

Commotion at the door. Shouting, pushing, punching.
What's going on? Flailing arms, furious faces, brutality in
action. They're hitting each other. Someone's lying on the
floor, their face all bloody, blood's gushing out of their
face forming a gleaming red puddle in front of them. Then
the kicking starts, they've got boots on. He's already
unconscious. They're going to kill him. Hey, come on,
that's enough.

Shut it, shut your mouth
you fucker, you fucking

Sorry
Fraid not
You can't come in

that's great
I'm gonna flatten you
you wanker, you ponce, you make me sick

does anybody
want to say something?
is anybody
trying to tell us something?
you got something
to say to me?
say it again
I can't hear you

To cut a long story short they storm the place,
split up and disperse among
the other guests. The police are already here.
The artist signs the policemen's truncheons.
The policemen have a glass of champagne.
The fighters look at the pictures.
Now the discussions start about what happened.
Was this life's attempt to break out
or art stepping out
from beyond the two dimensional and invading the

space?
Was it planned? Something really perverse?

and so the evening
gradually began to wind down
and for a brief respite people sat
on chairs and picked up a glass
and drank, a toast, a drop,
a glass, of wine, the wine

there was still wine left
and the last cigarette nowhere like being smoked
so people sat there, enveloped in thought
thinking nothing, people weren't thinking anything at that
time

I really liked that actually

9. THE BIG RECEPTION

Then everybody goes upstairs, into the flat
that's where the big reception is –
Huge rooms, flowers arranged in the corners
and art everywhere, loads of books,
the smell of prosperity and the same beautiful people as
before.
The view from the balcony stretches wide
across the city at night.

and we step out
onto the balcony
and the sky is above us
everything's rushing rushing in that direction
the rush of life and talk

they touch briefly on money
again here, after all
none of this would be possible
without money or rich people
who are willing to spend their money on art

what do these collectors actually buy?
do they buy things like this?
or an object like that?
a work of art?
what benefit does the buyer get from owning it?
can they buy the spirit behind it too?

of course
because they're paying for their desire
to be wild and totally free
someone with no boundaries
who undermines
the status quo
with the same money
they earn
for participating in it
it's no less absurd
than all that hypercritical criticism
or the artistic desire
finally just to say no
and remain completely outside

[and next door
in the next room
a lighter conversation
exulting once more in the splendid colours
here too there are pictures
scrutiny and impression
and the fairy tale from before
gets finished
the artist and the king
of course it finshes
on a topical note
about power
the way that being different from the opposition
and the power of art politicises people
in unseen, covert ways

while we mustn't forget
the flirting that's going on at the same time

in every corner, in every room
at every table, naturally, of course
because there are fantastic women there
and the men show what they've got
they look, chat, show off
crowing here, squawking there
and anyone who doesn't like it
can go]

Discussion about abstraction.
That endless conversation I keep having with Albert,
that painted pictures also have to be something more
than abstract pictures. Finished.
That it's not enough for art
to be so self-referential,
that only the most hardened experts
can appreciate the sensations
hiding within
the new painting.
That with every new picture
you've got to go through
the same old rubbish every time – as if
no one had ever painted anything before. That that
means
there's no such thing as achievement or progress
and nothing that's already been done.
That every picture, even abstracts, has to
deal naively in the sensory information of
visual facts. And that there are therefore
no solutions – for anything
that in its own way every picture is a completely new
opening of the eyes, first thing in the morning, not
knowing anything,
that only later becomes complex and awkward
broken, difficult, ruined, etc. etc.

no, ok, I'm sorry,
that goes without saying

thoughts can be real
they're just not objects

yeah, yeah yeah, yeah
'ts alright, 'ts alright

[right beside them
other people are talking about something else
he went to dinner
she was at the theatre
she asks about the football
he asks about people at work

fascinating
what you're not saying
yeah

in the next room
some people are even dancing
just a quick look
in this room of passion
for music
it's really loud
not much talking, nice

there's someone lying
on the floor
two, just lying there
that's funny
they're both lying there
on the floor they're even
moving a little
hang on
what's that?
what are they up to?
nice and dark here
nice and loud

what's the time?
how long?

now they look at each other
as if they're in love?
and dance again
really happy, crazy]

it's slowly starting to get emptier
this scene is coming to an end
this filmmaker's showing off a bit
that woman's a model, she's hanging on
his every word, she is
the junior dealer asks the assistant
whether the lawyer has already summonsed the other
side
of course, what he thinks is understandable,
it's just he thinks that in this case
sure, no, on the contrary, that's it,
oh right, well then, see you, you too

a dog barks quietly
and someone can be heard saying
I can hear
your heart beating my love
a theory of mistakes
in love

what did you say?

course
yeah
the full palette, sure

10. HE WHO DRANK NOTHING BUT WATER
THIS NIGHT

that's it
he can't take any more
he's off home
meetings all over the place
you meet up here, go on there
have such and such planned, course
the night's hardly begun yet and

you want the night to just carry you along
out
out where?
nobody knows, you'll find out
You'll see what happens
that's the difference
to the work of art here
in the room
that's never ever open
whatever happens
however it ends up
that's fixed
that's the death
of art
that it's already finished
and we aren't

11. LOOK

look
there

oh yeah

wow

ACT SIX

'hand on breast, 1990, 244 x 366'
– Jeff Koons

III: Palette

1. IN BED

Babe
not now
it's important
I'm busy
you make me sick
what?

it's over

2. OUTSIDE

let's get in there quick
come on
's freezing
's not
well I'm freezing
wimp

3. IN THE LOO

[I'm really pushing it today
me too]
I'm going to get so
wasted
yeah
so am I
sounds good
let's get started
yeah

right now
here

they have a drink
they prepare a line
they take it
they talk at each other
they take a bit more
cocaine

ah
ee

not bad
not half
yeah right
it's looking good
what did you say
just now?
what did you say?

doesn't matter

let's get back in there
shall we?
yeah sure
not bad
definitely not half bad

[4. PARRTY PARRTY PARRTY

What're you looking like that for?
me?
What's the matter?
what?
d'you want to take something?
no thanks
why not?
I've got some blinding pills here

honest?

have a look round
they're all my pills tonight
how much?
to you twenty
not cheap
hey mate
you know
what time it is?

no

how many then?
gives us ten
you got the two hundred?
there
be right back

5. CELLAR

Why's that man hitting
that woman?

Golden boy's
beating up some slag, why?
he hates her, but why?
she been cheating on him or something?
I don't know
those screams are for real
yeah
bad scene

what's the woman doing
with her hand?

naked woman
alone
fingering herself
no pleasure, angry, businesslike
bored with herself
and the idea
of just now briefly being hot for something

what exactly?
she makes a bit of an effort
there's a little wave of relief
can't really call it orgasm
she puts her hand under her nose
and smells

beautiful image
you call that beautiful?
what else is it?
dark, bitter, don't know
aha

I can hardly recognize you
it's great
it's not?
why not?
don't know

can I pay to use your hand?
where did that come from?
they way you're standing here
what way?
sorry, excuse me

twenty?
yeah
you must be joking
thirty? fifty, forty
look just piss off
I'm not

great big beautiful woman
shaving
one leg up
on a stool
all covered in white
great
bending over
nonchalantly
concentrating hard

on what she's doing
the television's on
Harald Schmidt
applause
the telephone rings
the woman looks up

some bloke with a phone in his hand
and in the other he's got
his thing
he's wanking
and talking and listening
so what?

a man with shit on his pants
and a million dollars
wrapped in barbed wire
caught
motionless
piercing gaze
beside him Maggie Rizer
showing him her armpits
the little hills
really sexy

naked woman on a sofa
her hand in her lap
quite calm
look
a little dog
curled up at her feet
the folds of cloth
the bright cushions
in the depths of the trunk at the back
the maid's unnaked female back
a tree, a pillar, the evening sky

woman screaming
bickering, bellowing, cursing
her voice escalating hysterically
quite piercing

man
standing turned away
frozen
dazed
he's waiting

he's going to bleed for that
we'll see
I'm not afraid any more
with whose money?
broken man, broken woman

young woman with dove's feather
old woman: desolation

suicide picture
in yellow and purple
madmen in the streets
a plan with no goal
letters
everything the wrong way round
bodies torn apart
in pieces
almost everything ruined

she mumbles strange things
no one knows
who to?
can't understand
what?
the way she looks
the way she walks
a last human
at the last moment
woman
child
made
desire
he can't remember

before
on the way here
I completely lost my head
that's wonderful
no
it's terrible
it's horrifying, really

really?

Openness, lack of protection, precision
banal, magnificent and tragically trashilly normal
images of images, moments, melodies

May I? what?
fuck you?, just a moment
what for? because he needs a bit
why's he snorting like that?
he's so excited, why?
because of me, honestly? yeah
that's cool, well, right, what is it?
you can now, is he ready? yeah
ok, come here then, how?
like this, like this?, that's it
and this goes
yeah?
we put that in here
why?, cos that's where it belongs, oh
hm, what? That feels good
think so too
ah
what are you shouting like that for?
because then I enjoy it more
and then? then you'll come too
and then? and then it's the next one's turn
is it? yeah, pity, why's it a pity?
it was nice, you mean, we're never going to do it
again?, but we just did
still, once more, but the others

all want to too
oh? yeah, pity
that was really nice
yeah

he does the deal
pays the money
takes the goods
away from here
away

drunken man hits woman
the same image yet again
please don't wipe it away
why not?
it belongs here too
I hate that
I don't want to see that

drunken man
hits his woman
does she belong to him?
really stupid question, so
drunken man hits woman in the house,
comes home, locks the door, etc.

you've got better boobs
than her
you think so?
yeah
I like that
so do I

are you
a mother the same as
her over there?
more or less
what's her name?
and that?

motif at the other end of the floor
abstract story
image
of the present
wait opposite, then

wrecks, people too
all of them?
always?
only? till when?
why? what for? how did that happen?
suddenly?, the man's
desire for
who he
and of course
hers for him too

course, that's enough
got it, that's it
abused, destroyed
treated, too weak
from this ambition and that one
of horror and doing
trial in the face
the script of the ancients

the verdict lost
and forgotten and destroyed
normal story
of course, no question

last scene, cellar
last image here, quick

guy at a desk, pen in hand
stands up, writes, stands up again, paces up and down
writes, books on the floor, papers, everything there full
head bowed, writing like that, nods
and stands up again
paces up and down, talks, he talks all the time

writes what he says, nods as he writes
writes as he speaks, nods with his head
bounces his knee, writes what he hears
hears what he thinks, thinks what he sees
images, out of words, a matter of silence
and noise, very loud noise]

6. DANCING

if it's not wild
then what's the point?
forget it
if it doesn't take off
then why bother?
if it won't fly
of its own volition
doesn't matter
if she's not there
because she doesn't like it
forget it
if she doesn't want
what you thought
he's waiting and hoping

and then when she does come
the way she is, how is she?
yeah, there, that's where she was
just now, beautiful

forget it.

7. AT THE BAR

er, uh
uh uh
what?
a drink?
what?
could we have something
else to drink?

we're closing now
are you?
already?
you know what time
it is?
no
that figures

[8. RIGHT BESIDE THEM

the Mercedes does what?
it's brand new, isn't it?
right beside them, stone cold sober both of them,
talking their heads off, the music's too loud
Mercedes, Acropolis, artworks by Meier,
history, that book, this play,
the Getty, the what?

the whole thing, time
this joy of ours today
thinking emotions
not you too
maybe that's good though
isn't it?

9. ON THE FLOOR

shall we get up?
nah, what for?
it's great down here
let's skin up another one
good idea
did you have the gear
or me
dunno
have a look
what did I do with it?
hm
good question

have we got any
coke left?

nah

shall we buy some more?
is he still there?
I thought he'd gone again
the guy
with the cocaine
shall I go and have a look?

nah

let's skin up again
yeah
don't rush it
not now
give me the gear
I thought you had the gear
yeah?
me?
hmm?]

10. AT THE DOOR

now what?
yeah
now what?
back to mine?
or back to mine?
go to yours

mine's
disgustingly antisocial

so's mine
who fucking cares
crash out
watch videos
yeah

then go to sleep
together

look
at this light
bit too bright almost
nice though
I think

you're right
shall we go then

yeah, go on

11. IN BED

Babe
yeah
I love you
sssh

12. SO GREAT

like before

they fuck
they shag
they do it
they get it on

kisses
they shriek
they go silent and laugh
they trash everything
and I mean
everything

course
I understand
that's good
so great

RAINALD GOETZ

but then
then
but then then

ACT SEVEN

'on overgrown paths' – Hamsun

V: The Picture

1. VISION

then I went out

suddenly it was silent
and this silence

quiet
inside me too
and I held my breath

I stopped, I listened
and thought: yeah
great now, this sudden quietness
the silence coming at me
from this lack of words

weird, people, you know
the stuff you do, everything
the way you live, there's so much
how you can stand
up to it all, just one person,
an individual, how
how can you do it?
resisting that power
who's capable of that?

who's there?
inside me?
this figure
who does and achieves so much, who's always
producing, making statements, usually without a sound,
cool

these questions aren't thought so much
as felt, nodding
that it's beautiful it's like this
amazed for a little while
I mean, you so rarely think about it
well you don't do you
normally

so I was outside
and it was morning
and this silence now
it was unbelievable
and I took a breath and kept walking
kept on nodding, really happy inside
feeling mellow

it was good
one day and three nights
the seven pictures in the gallery
not too big, just right
so when you see them you go
yeah, that's nice

that's how it was, sometimes it works
and sometimes it doesn't
still full of secrets
the depths of the creative soul

yeah

and I could see
the world in front of me
an art, I could see a painting that
I could see people's faces
people like us, the same
only different because they're talking
breaking, arguing and
losing and winning again
new

the same processes
in every one, each individual, all of them
weird, great, just don't
make too much of it, this gentle moment
of wonder, no

you can see the point
of disagreement, the edge, the end
the hatred, the tidal wave of stupidity
drowning everything, the decline and
fall, interruption, fragmentation and

what we all
know, know only too well
negativity, the carping, the attacks, rejection,
reactions of disgust, total
non-stop, some kind of in-built
reflex, like there's nothing else but that: nothing

yeah: nothing but no
absolute and constant
and nothing else, and
you know it's wrong
what happens, your reaction, you're desperate
for anything that isn't no, I'm sorry
it's that simple, yeah
and if you don't like it you can
yeah, what? what then?
go?

and I could see that there in front of the pictures it
yes what was it like there, was it good?
it was good, there
it was good there
I liked being there

there was accuracy and reassurance
and more than you can understand
there was intensity, power, a wholeness, an incredible
amount

said
and at the same time silence
it was all there
together somehow

I'm alone again in the gallery
the party's over and the glasses and ashtrays
've been cleared away into a corner
and the pictures radiate
from every direction, the excitement
they create
and yet their gentleness
stored in my memory
their glowing and whispering, their coming, their call

tragic too
a feeling generally
of how far we've got
and still so young
what lies before us, everything

and he could see that
I watched him sigh, nod and go
and then I went home
back home
pretty tired now
and I could hear my heart going
ba dum, ba dum
I stopped
just for a moment
and listened